M000210930

We

Who

Laugh,

Last

Julia T. Thomason
Walt Grebing

NATIONAL MIDDLE SCHOOL ASSOCIATION

nmsa

NATIONAL MIDDLE SCHOOL ASSOCIATION

This special publication of humorous incidents and stories was conceived by Julia Thomason and Walt Grebing. These two experienced middle level educators organized the incidents selected from among invited submissions into the seven categories which comprise this collection.

Dr. Thomason is a Professor of Curriculum and Instruction at Appalachian State University, Boone, North Carolina and the 1989-90 President of the National Middle School Association. Walt Grebing is the Principal of Broomfield Heights Middle School in the Boulder Valley School District, Broomfield, Colorado, frequently cited as an exemplary middle school.

The Association appreciates their efforts in bringing the lighter side of middle level education to the profession at large. Thanks too to the many educators who willingly shared bits of their experiences. Unfortunately all could not be included and some identifying information was not available.

Illustrations are by Julia S. Seerley.

Copyright © 1990 by the National Middle School Association
4807 Evanswood Drive, Columbus, Ohio 43229

$5.00 (NMSA members)

Printed in the United States of America by
Panaprint, Inc., P. O. Box 10297, Macon, Ga 31297

ISBN: 1-56090-053-9

Contents

Dedication

To my dad, Charles Tiller, whose sense of humor has been a very important part of my life. Thank you for such a wonderful inheritance.

Julia

To my daughters, Marci and Kara, whose antics in the middle school help me to see the importance of humor both as a father and as a principal.

Walt

INTRODUCTION

Throughout our personal careers, we have always
believed that a sense of humor is essential for both
happiness and success in teaching. Once we found
ourselves teaching at the middle level, we were even more
convinced. Without this ability to laugh at ourselves and
the situations we find ourselves in, we are doomed to spend
untold hours in misery, often at the mercy of clever
seventh graders who have that uncanny ability to "get our
goat." Of course, in terms of getting our goat, some of us
have the uncanny ability to let students figure out
immediately where we have tied it.

Both of us have stories about occasions when we let
the students completely destroy our professional demeanors
with the most innocent-seeming remarks. We can both
remember students coming out with words, answers, and
opinions that were not what we meant to say at all, but,
indeed, were classic near-misses. We thought we had heard
all the excuses and have spent many evenings laughing
about the humor (for adults) in youth's passage through
puberty. We certainly have had our goats gotten; and we
are convinced we are not alone. So we asked people we
knew, people we worked with, people who came to
conferences, and people we just happened to run into on the
street, if they had stories like ours. It is no surprise that
everyone had a story. If fact, hasn't every teacher and
principal said, at one time or another, I should have written
a book? Within all of us who work with middle level
students there is a best seller full of these crazy things the
kids say and do. Each of us could have written a book.

1

Well, this is that book written with all due respect and in honor of those who are so busy doing the marvelous work of instructing middle grades students that they have not had the time to write their own. We have been collecting these stories over the last eighteen months from people all across the country, and even other countries. We have given credit in every case we could to the contributors and their schools. We have smiled, giggled, even laughed out loud as we worked to pull together this special publication. And in the process we have confirmed once again that *we who laugh, last.*

Julia Thomason
Walt Grebing

1. A MATTER OF MIDDLE SCHOOL

Ask someone what working in a middle school is like and you will get really great responses such as the following: "Teaching in a middle school is like being a zookeeper in charge of the health, well-being, comfort and productivity of the animals." "Teaching in a middle school is like working with thirty hand grenades with their pins half-pulled. "It's like trying to teach a gland." "It's like being in the middle of a battle zone and you've lost your red cross." "It's like being a fairy godmother to Godzilla." "It's a combination of R-rated movies and Smurf stories."

It's just a matter of middle school.

I wouldn't have missed it for the world

Arriving at the afternoon dance... dressed to the hilt ... cologne/aftershave... more than abundant! Eighth graders being constantly reminded that back pockets are not for the hands of your partner on the dance floor. Seventh graders dancing...maybe actually moving two whole steps during the entire song...never, never making eye contact (something would have to be said). Also, seventh grade "friends" walking behind making silly faces and rolling their eyes. Sixth graders running in ever-decreasing concentric circles until they punched a girl! What glee! What glee!

At its conclusion, 400 sweaty bodies vowing to do it all again...soon!

—*Larry Lewis, Mansfield Public Schools, Mansfield, OH*

The yokes on you ...

All seventh grade students were asked to bring a hard-boiled egg to science class. We were going to cut them into sections to resemble the different layers of the earth.

The lab went well until third period when in walks a student wearing a pretty dress and carrying her egg.

Although forgetful, she remembered her egg. I was really pleased. I gave the instructions and students began to slice their eggs into sections.

Walking about the room, I noticed this student had her egg in her hand. I was about to remind her to cut the egg on the table when she cut into the egg and the raw yoke dropped into her lap — she remembered the egg, but forgot to boil it!

— *Jim DiAngelous, Roosevelt School, Kingsburg, CA*

A mixed message

We keep a notebook of the children's work and I was punching holes in their papers when I thought that if I had another hole punch, the students could help. So I sent a student down to my co-worker's class to borrow one. The student, excited about going, went into the classroom and requested "the hole punch." My colleague thought she said "the whole bunch." Since my student was so excited, the teacher immediately had her students line up and come to my classroom. As I looked up from working with students on their notebooks into my room marched the other class. They proceeded to sit down with a look of excitement. They were expecting something out of the ordinary. I was only expecting a "hole punch." Anyway, a great laugh was a perfect ending for our hectic week.

— Toni Carter, South Mesa Elementary,
Pueblo, CO

Impossible?

Our sixth graders go on a four-day backpack trip in West Virginia each spring. It is a fairly spartan experience — tents, sleeping bags, unpredictable weather, and no bathrooms. To help prepare each upcoming 6th grade class, I ask those who have completed the trip to write letters to next year's campers.

One letter included the following admonition: "You're probably worried about going to the bathroom outside for four days. Don't ask me. I didn't go."

— Ruth Huyler Glass, The Langley School,
McLean, VA

It all happened so fast...

As a middle school administrator, I was involved in a most interesting discipline case. One morning an irate parent called me to report that her daughter had been sexually harassed or molested on the school bus. She indicated that this particular young man had attempted to make advances toward her daughter and had been aggressive to the point of even tearing the front of her sweater. I too became concerned and immediately investigated the matter.

After an exhaustive session with the two young people involved, the following story unfolded. They were good friends. She had a crush on him and thought he was cute. He wore one of the passing fad hairstyles with long strands of hair flowing down the nape of his neck. While riding the bus, the girl asked if she could braid these strands of hair. He accepted her invitation and laid his head in her lap. During the braiding process one thing led to another and he decided to become more familiar with her torso. However, during his exploration his braces became entangled in her sweater. In the process of untangling braces from the material, the sweater became torn. The young lady, afraid that her mother would be angry about the torn sweater, developed the story about being harassed to explain the damage to the sweater.

When the truth came to the surface, I was very much relieved and contacted the mother. She was not overly enthused with the truth and suggested some punishment. Such is life in the middle school.

> — *Walter Richardson, Indianola Middle School, Columbus, OH*

Snake charmer

Billy was charming, but academics eluded him. However, when I discovered his special interest in snakes I found the key that when exploited permitted him to make progress. One of my contracts with him even resulted in my having to hold one of his snakes, for he read the agreed-on number of books.

After leaving my eighth grade he often returned for a visit always bringing a snake to show the students and inform them about that snake's habits. During one visit he told me about his job at a local pet shop. Subsequently I went to the store to tell the manager what a good job Billy did in helping students overcome their fear of snakes and to suggest that he might visit other schools with his message.

As we talked in the shop Billy had a large boa and was playing with it. Suddenly we noticed a policeman ticketing my car out front, for I had parked in the wrong place. Billy ran out of the store, the snake around his neck, to talk to the policeman. The snake was writhing wildly. The policeman ran around his car and jumped in. Billy leaned down to talk to him and the snake started to enter the patrol car! The last we saw of the policeman, he was careening through the parking lot screaming, "Tell her she can park anywhere she wants tooooooo!"

— Jeanne Ballard, Apopka Middle School, Longwood, FL

The giveaway

It was devastating to find her grade book which had included the key for the upcoming test had been taken. Mrs. McGuire never expected to see it again. "How," she wondered, "am I going to remember all those grades?" Her prayers were answered as she graded the next day's test. In her 4th period class, one of the students answered a question with the brilliant notion that "Answers may vary." Guess who had the book?

— Barbara Lamb, Apopka Memorial
Middle School, Longwood, FL

Quick-change artist

The object of the activity was to decide on a word to spell after a topic is given, run to a pile of mixed up letters (piles consisting of the alphabet and one extra set of vowels), have each student grab a needed letter, run back to the line, and in correct order, hold their letters up to spell their word. One team figured out the short words were winners, as far less time was needed to find letters and arrange them. One topic was "something here at the school." The group ran to the pile and pulled out the letters W E. The other group challenged by saying, "What if everyone is absent?" The girl holding the "W" flipped it around and new word was M E.

— Unknown contributor

8

Great minds ...

A collection of particularly enthusiastic and bright kids were enrolled in my health class. One was a very tiny and very achievement-oriented youngster. (The kind who asks for extra credit on the first day.) I always attempted to reduce his obsession with grades by referring to his brilliance.

On stethoscope day, I suggested they listen to each other's hearts and lungs. In the midst of this activity, I noticed several students standing over my grade-conscious student. They had their stethoscopes pressed to his head and were describing the sound of his "brilliance" as they heard him read his homework assignment.

— *Jim Snodgrass, Sepulveda Jr. High*

It's a small world

My own daughter, Monica, was asked to write about Dr. Martin Luther King's statement, "I have a dream." She wrote, "I have a dream. A dream that someday all kids will play together. Even kids from different classrooms."

— Unknown contributor

Media messages

On the historic occasion of the space shuttle Discovery's first return to Earth, several sixth-grade classes were in my room to watch the touchdown on television. We discussed the problems of reentry and were entranced by the skillful landing.

For the students, however, the loudest cheers were on hold, awaiting the astronauts' emergence from the shuttle. The protestations were uniformly strong when told that this would not happen for an hour — long after they were in their next class. Trying to hurry history, as only this TV generation can do, one frustrated, but hopeful, youngster turned to me and said, "Mrs. Berrington, can't they do instant replay now?"

— Susan Berrington, Owen Brown Middle School, Columbia, MD

Incredible shrinking teacher

Terry, an outgoing 7th grader, waltzed into my class one morning, looked me over, and said, "Mrs. Cox, did you get your hair cut? You look shorter today."

How typical of middle level students!

— Susan K. Cox, York Middle School,
York, NE

Ignorance is contagious

The teacher suspected that Jimmy was cheating but had difficulty proving it even though his answers had a remarkable similarity to his friend, Eddie's. The conclusive proof came when Jimmy's answer to question #17 was, "I don't know, either."

— Dorothy Skinner (Submitted by Winona Skaggs),
Sequoyah Middle School, Edmond, OK

Sounds like ...

One youngster was acting out a charade in front of the class. His instructions read, "You are sneaking into the kitchen for a midnight snack." He had hardly begun creeping across the front of the room when students began to yell possible answers. Exasperated, he broke the "charade code" of silence and exclaimed, "Hush. I'm not even to the refrigerator yet."

— Mary Obsner, Green Brook High School,
Green Brook, NJ

Joy on a skewer

I recall vividly that hurried Monday morning in October, 1988. My preparation for Period 1 Language was almost complete. Although my task was interrupted by "good mornings" and "How was your weekend, Mrs. Robertson?" from the 7th and 8th graders who occupied our wing, I was feeling good about what I was accomplishing.

However, my progress and concentration were broken when Joy arrived. I felt a tap on my shoulder and as I turned around I was greeted with a warm smile and a one-armed hug from this sweet 7th grader.

"Mrs. Robertson, I made a present for you. It will start your day off right," said Joy. Secretly hoping that the "surprise" would not be something alive, slimy, or against the school rules, I said, "How nice of you." From behind her back, Joy revealed "it." I peered down at it and my eyes searched for some meaning. Before me was a construction of leaves and a stick piercing the center of each leaf.

I vowed not to ask the heartless question. Luckily Joy asked it for me. "You don't know what it is, do you?" I had to confess that I didn't and humbly responded, "Why don't you tell me." Pride rushed over Joy's face and she

12

said, "It's a leaf kabob!" We both laughed until tears came to our eyes. Joy was right, this "middle school moment" had started my day off just right!

— Laurie Aboudara-Robertson, Redwood Middle School, Napa, CA

Signs of the times

Students were asked to list the five things they would bring along, other than adequate food, clothing, and shelter, if they were to live on an isolated island for one year.

Boys:		Girls:	
(1)	Satellite Dish	(1)	Radio
(2)	TV	(2)	Boyfriend
(3)	Girl	(3)	Telephone
(4)	Descrambler for TV dish	(4)	Tapes
(5)	Jet Ski	(5)	Hot Tub

— Alan Burke & Joe Kilby, Orting Middle School

Long-term planning

One of my students was completing an end of the year assignment called "When I grow up, I want to be....." with the following results:

at 15—a movie star
at 18—married
at 21—moved out of the house
at 25—a football player
at 35—a rock star
at 50—cheat on my wife

— Christine E. Perry, Sierra Vista, AZ

2. PROBABLY IT'S PUBERTY

The passage from childhood through adolescence on the way to adulthood is "fraught with marauders" as W.C. Fields once said. It is rarely a smooth trip and it certainly does not happen overnight. Kids don't walk into class one day and announce, "Hey, I've pubed." They have to make error after error and be embarrassed time after time as they struggle through the perils of puberty. They try out things just to see what fits. They make errors in judgement, like trying to neck on the back of the band bus or holding hands with someone who months (or days) later they will deem to be a perfect gross-out. They have to wear outrageous clothes, put makeup on with a putty knife, wear so much green eyeshadow you think their gallbladders have burst, or massage three facial hairs that may someday, sometime (but not now) become a real mustache. In other words, they have to be perfectly normal. In fact, almost always, when we hear, "I wish that child would act his age!," he is.

Remember the one you first had a "thing" for — the elaborate preparations you made to be in the right place at the right time? Remember zits — and parents so out of touch they were downright Neanderthals — teachers who could not possibly have ever been young? Remember the ups and downs, the highs and lows, the unexplainable everythings? Probably it was just puberty.

These anecdotes point out to us once again, just how tough it is to be thirteen. The uncanny thing, for us at least, is just how astute the students are about their own predicament. They seem often to have a better handle on the whole situation than we give them credit for. They seem to somehow know more than we do....or at least they surely seem to know more than we did at that age.

Well, why not?

In my eighth grade French class, I do a clothing and color unit where students learn the vocabulary for various items of clothing and ten or eleven colors. An oral project in this class is in the form of a fashion show. Students go in front of the class and describe their clothing in French, of course. As his final item to describe, one young boy dropped his pants to describe his underwear to the class! The class was as shocked and surprised as I was!

— Nancy McKnight, Ingomar Middle School, Pittsburgh, PA

She knows herself

After being asked to pick up a paper she dropped, the student cried, "I'm tired of cleaning up after myself!"

— Simcha Saul, Valley Alternative Magnet , Los Angeles Unified School District

Reason enough

On the second day of school, a new boy was found crying. He said that he had a headache and stomach ache and wanted to go home. We finally found out that he had put his lunch, notebook, math book, and TURTLE in the wrong locker and couldn't get at them.

—James A. Zeedyk, Holland Junior High School, Holland Public Schools

Embarrassing innocence —
or mother didn't tell the whole story

On Halloween day almost all our faculty and many of the students dress in costume. One Halloween I dressed as the absent minded professor, with mismatched shoes and socks, plaid pants and shirt, shirt buttoned crooked and hanging out, etc. For added effect, I had lined in wrinkles on my face and had put white pigment in my hair to make it look gray. During the day there was a lot of good natured kidding by students with comments like, "Mr. Shaw, I see that you washed the dye out of your hair." or "Why didn't you wear a costume Mr. Shaw?" However, I was not prepared for what happened at fifth period. As the class came in, one seventh grade girl pointed at me, let out a high pitched laugh and shrieked, "Mr. Shaw, it looks like pubic hair!"

The students looked stunned and I responded with a sharp "What!?"

"It does! It looks just like pubic hair!" she repeated in a loud laughing voice.

"Sally, that's enough!" I reprimanded. "See me after class."

At the end of class she was standing there saying, "You wanted to see me?"

"Yes," I said. "I think your comments at the first of class were very inappropriate."

"What do you mean?" she asked with a puzzled look on her face.

16

"That is not an appropriate way for a young girl to be talking," I explained.

"But Mr. Shaw, I didn't swear. I never swear."

At this point I began to realize what the problem was. "Sally, do you know what pubic hair is?" I asked.

"Sure," she stated confidently. "My mom told me about it. She said that as people get older, they get pubic hair. It's just gray hair."

Not knowing what else to do at this point, I did what Miss Neff, my seventh grade teacher, would have done. "Go look it up in the dictionary," I suggested.

The dictionary was little help. "It says, 'hair about the pubic region.' What does that mean, Mr. Shaw?" she asked.

I was caught. I didn't know what else to do. After a pause, I finally said, "Sally, that's the hair between your legs."

Her mouthed dropped open, her eyes widened, and there was a second of shocked silence followed by a protracted "GROOOOOSSSS!!" Then came the embarrassed, "Oh, Mr. Shaw, I'm sorry," followed by a muttered, angry, "My mother should have told me!!"

I always wondered what happened that night when her mother asked her what she learned in school that day.

— Terry Shaw, Irving Middle School, Norman, OK

Till tomorrow do us part

This little tidbit helps to remind me of who I'm dealing with when I work with young people and of the world I passed through but am no longer absorbed in.

While listening to a popular rock station, I heard a young girl call in a request for a special song. "Could you play a special song for my boyfriend?" the teenager asked. "It's our anniversary."

"Sure," replied the disc jockey. "How many years have you been going together?"

Her reply? "One week."

To be young is to see forever as now.

forever and a week !

— *Judi C. Oehler, Director,*
Red Cross Youth Services, Dallas, TX

It's all in how you look at it

It was time for our sports physical examination and some of the boys had never had one before so they stood in line chattering nervously. When the doctor arrived, he scolded the boys for being noisy and told them to get ready by stripping to the waist. When he looked up from his papers, he saw one confused boy with his hand up. When the doctor asked him what his question was, the boy replied, "Which way?"

— John Rowley, Heritage Junior High,
Livingston, NY

It's probably catching

Paul, a sixth grader, never seemed to have an answer to a teacher's direct question. One day, however, he came through. To begin the Sex-Ed unit of the health curriculum, I asked "Does anyone know what the word puberty means?" Paul's hand shot up. He was stretching, waving, and yelling "Oh, oh! I know! I know!" How could I not call on Paul? "Yes, Paul, do you know what puberty means?" "Well, I don't know the meaning, but my mom took me to the doctor and he said I have it."

— Mary Hausermann, Leslie Middle School,
Salem, Oregon

Are you sure?

Several years ago, in our sixth grade sex education unit, I led a discussion of the changes that occur to boys and girls as they mature — pubic hair, breast development, deeper voice. As I mentioned the growth spurt, a little hand, belonging to the smallest boy in the class, shot up. With desperation in his voice, he pleaded, "When?"

— George Thomas, Moorestown Friends School, Moorestown, NJ

Sexy computers

My 7th grade computer students were required to write a movie review about computer topics recently. One student's lead-in was, "...it was about output, input, and DATING PROCESSING."

— Mrs. Jayne A. Kasten, Holman Middle School, St. Ann, MO

I'm right, right?

AIDS pre-test 8th grade — Question on oral sex:

Teacher discussion: Do you understand this question?
Student response: "Yes, that is when you talk about it!"

— Lynda Durnil, Thomas Jefferson Middle School, Decatur, IL

Take it a step further

We were discussing the differences between pessimists and optimists. To further clarify the two meanings, I used the old "water glass" example.

"An optimist," I said, "would say that the glass is half full, while the pessimist would say what?"

"A pessimist," Joe replied, "would say that it was half full of poison!"

> — *Alex Zemansky, Gregory Middle School, Naperville, IL*

3. ISN'T THAT WHAT I THOUGHT I SAID I MEANT?

In helping teachers know what to expect of middle grade students' thinking processes, we stress being alert for off-the-track reasoning. Often ideas that sound wonderful in the brain, sound really off the wall when they come out of the mouth. Many times, ideas and concepts that students have never seen in print, must suddenly be spelled out, or ideas that have only been seen in print must be pronounced.

The results can be, and often are, hilarious. The real trick, then, is to laugh when laughter will release the tension or to ignore the whole thing when that seems to be the best tactic. How do middle grades teachers know which strategy to use? They just know, that's all. And that's why they get the big bucks, right?

Voice, tense, tension

Teacher: How do you know if a verb is in the active or passive voice?

Student: When a verb is in the active voice, its subject shows some action. When a verb is in the passive voice, its subject shows some passion.

— *Nanny J. Simmons, Director of Curriculum, Fort Worth, TX*

Hear, hear!

Teacher to student:

"Johnny, you should concentrate harder."

Johnny several days later, very excited,

"Teacher, teacher, I'm concentrated."

— Janet Lee Banks, Pittsburgh, PA

It says so right here!

A student arrived at the principal's office irate that the teacher had marked one question on a social studies test wrong. While practicing personally inviting behaviors, the principal asked, "What's the problem?"

"I'm right! I know I'm right," declared the student. Whereupon the text was ripped open to a page and a slender finger touched upon the point of disagreement.

On a fill-in-the-blank geography test a question was asked regarding the term — allspice. The student reading the question had written in the word "hence" as the answer. He pointed to the paragraph in the text to verify his answer. It read:

"Allspice is a particularly unique spice, as it blends the qualities of a number of popular spices, hence its name."

— Larry Lewis, Mansfield Public Schools,
Mansfield, OH

Reason enough

After studying *A Christmas Carol*, a student answered this question.

"Why did Scrooge's father hold a grudge against him?"

"His father didn't like Scrooge because while the mother was having birth with Scrooge she died."

> — *Jean Buttz, Thomas Jefferson Junior High, Decatur, IL*

Doesn't everybody know?

My favorite story comes from a sixth grade boy who was taking his turn at reporting current events.

"In Belfast, Northern Ireland a young Catholic schoolboy was leaving a dance and was attacked and beaten by a gang of roving prostitutes."

"John", I interrupted, "are you absolutely sure of your facts?"

"Oh, Mrs. Jones", the student responded with obvious impatience. "Of course, I am sure. Everyone knows the Catholics are fighting the prostitutes in Northern Ireland!"

> — *Catherine Funk, Principal, Taipei American School, Shihlin, Taipei, Taiwan*

It just came off, I guess

One of our teachers was out of school for a month with a detached retina. A student explained this to the counselor by saying, "Mr. B. is out of school because of a detached rectum."

— Arlene Kaiser-Carson, Self Esteem Center, Fremont, California

A grammar lesson?

Just before CTBS Week this year, my 7th grade language arts students were reviewing punctuation marks and their uses. Not quite believing my ears, I moved over closer to Donna and clearly heard her instructing herself as she punctuated a page of lengthy sentences: "comma, comma, semi-condom, semi-condom, comma, semi-condom, semi-condom, comma, comma".

— Mary Jo Donlan, Zuni Middle School, Zuni, NM

Phonetically speaking

From an original sentence written by an 8th grader.

During the Middle Ages large populations were wiped out by the blue bonnet plague.

— Paulette Culpepper, Rosemont Middle School, Fort Worth, TX

As they see it

Mrs. Sandy Southern's class was discussing a recent North Carolina State Fair. She had just mentioned that then President Jimmy Carter had appeared on the opening day of the fair. One very enthusiastic youngster obviously in awe said, "I didn't know the rides were that good this year."

— Mary Obsner, Green Brook, NJ

When basketball is king

Once a week, we would play a current events game with questions on the past week's events. One particular question dealt with the NAACP which had been in the headlines. When Stephanie was asked this question, she showed a bit of "acronymical" confusion.

"The NAACP?" she echoed. "I don't know anything about college basketball!"

— Alex Zemansky, Gregory Middle School, Naperville, IL

He's a wheel watcher

One day the class and I were going over vocabulary words preliminary to reading our selection. I asked the students for the meaning of the word *misfortune*. One bright lad, without hesitation, said, "Vanna White!"

— Elizabeth Lee, Pueblo, CO

It seemed the manly thing to do

When I read the following definition on a final test I could hardly contain myself. I flew to the office to share it with my team.

Question: Identify the following: 1. Peter Abelard

Answer: Peter Abelard was a church man who was castrated for having a child out of wedlock.

— *Stephen Schell, Poudre High School, Fort Collins, CO*

It all adds up

The students in a self-paced special program would receive a worksheet, instruction booklet, and an audio tape to assist their progress. As their assignments were checked and approved they could proceed to the next level. This was done by my aide or myself.

One morning, while the students were busy working, my aide and I were discussing why Tom was absent. She informed me he had had a reaction to his medication and had nausea and swelling.

One student working in close proximity to our conversation looked up, removed his head phones, and asked, "Who's swellin' up from multiplication?"

— *Gayle Murray, West Millbrook Middle School, Raleigh, NC*

What's that you said?

When asked to fill in an information card at the first of the school year, students listed any visual or hearing problems. Joann, a seventh-grader, responded: "I do have a hearing problem, but I'm getting AIDS tomorrow."

— Laura Headley, Jackson Middle School,
Titusville, FL

Never turn your back

As a part of a dictionary unit one student was responsible for writing a new word on the board each day while the other students were to look up the word in their desk dictionaries. Since I was distributing papers, I did not notice the word that very shy Harold was writing on the board. When finished with the papers I turned to the board to see that today's word was *nymphomania.*

— Janet McKenzie, Caron Middle School,
North Allegheny Schools, PA

4. IT HELPS TO BE AS SQUIRRELY AS THE KIDS

Middle school teachers are probably not born that way. They may not even be made that way. We really aren't sure what makes someone in otherwise good mental health deliberately choose to teach at a level of schooling guaranteed to reduce you to your lowest common denominator. Maybe it's the answer to the question "Do you teach your subject to the kids or do you teach kids about your subject?" Maybe it's a genuine desire to have people stop you in the supermarket and console you about the dire circumstances under which you are subjected to making a living.

Whatever it is, middle grades teachers no longer seem to be waiting for someone up at the high school to die so a good job will open up there. They are no longer taking more than their fair share of leave days because middle grades kids make their teachers sicker than any other age group. They are no longer performing the great sham that Paul George refers to in tricking the kids by teaching them eleventh grade content in the seventh grade and holding the Woodrow Wilson Memorial Chair of Seventh Grade Social Studies. They are not the ones who show up for school in the morning looking like they won first prize in the barium enema contest.

They are in the middle grades by choice. At some point, they looked at twelve year olds and said, "I choose you!" At some point, sooner or later, these outstanding teachers recognized that child-centered practices probably are acceptable, that the social worker face is essential, and that it helps to be just as squirrely as the kids.

It sure looked funny to me

During the course of a discussion on elected state officials in a ninth grade government course, we came to Attorney General. That office was added to the now substantial list on the chalkboard. After a thoroughly satisfying discussion, one hand remained timidly in the air.

"Yes, Jake," I said in anticipation of his usual insightful contribution.

"Mr. Knierim, just what is a `horney general'?"

Shocked, I looked at the board to see written "ATTORNEY GENERAL." My printing had made the A-T-T look like A-H. The class and I joined Jake in a round of affirmation of his deep perceptivity and one upmanship on the teacher.

I regularly hear from members of that class. To the person they remember "Attorney General."

— *Willie Knierim, Social Studies Teacher, Boulder, CO*

Candid camera

One morning during the school announcements, the principal said: "Will the boy in the 2nd row in Mrs. Lamb's room sit down. Now!" Michael, who had been moseying along the row, quickly sat down in the first available seat. All eyes snapped to the box on the ceiling as though a camera were there. Students wondered aloud where the camera was hidden. To this day, all I have to do if a student misbehaves is to look up at the intercom. Silence immediately ensues.

— *Barbara Lamb, Apopka Memorial Middle School, Longwood, FL*

Have another one!

It is never a good idea to confiscate contraband and retain it in the office refrigerator. At our annual homeroom Christmas party a student brought a 2 liter bottle of Coke — laced with alcohol. After I got it from the student, I put it in the office refrigerator. We never seem to get around to cleaning out the contents so the Coke remained there.

Later, one of our office secretaries had a birthday and, as is our practice, we had an office party for her. We had cake and a 2 liter bottle of Coke. What we didn't know was that the secretary had selected the incorrect bottle and had actually given everyone, including our student assistant, the laced Coke. The student was quite religious and very opposed to alcohol in any form, but she only commented to the secretary that the Coke sure was good.

We almost had to bury the office secretary when she found out her error. To our knowledge, though, the office assistant never knew what hit her.

> — *Bonnie Lynch, El Dorado Middle School, El Dorado, KS*

Whatever it takes!

Joe, an intelligent, scholarly, yet athletic thirteen year old basketball player came over to the team huddle on a called time out and tried to ask the coach a question. The coach, preoccupied with his message to the team, put Joe off. Finally, as the team was being called out onto the court, Joe asked in desperation, "Coach, how many quarters in a ball game?" The coach, with a surprised look on his face, quipped back, "As many as it takes!"

> — *Daniel T. Erickson, Paw Paw Middle School, Paw Paw, MI*

As others see us

As the doctor prepared to look at my swollen, discolored ankle which I told him I had injured the previous day, he questioned me about the accident that necessitated my filing a workmen's compensation claim as an employee of the Volusia County School Board.

"How did you hurt your ankle?" he asked.

"I fell off a bus," I replied.

"Oh, you're a school bus driver?"

"No, I was on a field trip to Tallahassee" (He knew it was a 5-hour trip). "You went to Tallahassee and back yesterday?"

"No, I went to Tallahassee the day before yesterday and returned home last night."

"How many students did you have on this two-day field trip, and what age were they?"

When I told him that 65 seventh graders had gone to Tallahassee, he told me I was in the wrong place!

"What do you mean?" I asked.

"You obviously need your head examined, not your foot!"

— *Mary Beth Cowden, Southwestern Middle School, DeLand, Florida*

Tell it like it is

A colleague usually showed me the notes she was sending to parents to edit and proof. I wouldn't let her send the following note, but it reflects the frustrations we all feel as we work with children in the middle grades.

Dear Captain Jones,

I would appreciate it if you would speak with John. He is in a group by himself for math. In the past two weeks he has completed only two math assignments.

He "forgets" to listen. He "forgets" to do the assignment. He "forgets" to bring the assignment in.

If this continues, I am afraid I am going to "forget" to pass him.

— Christine E. Perry, Sierra Vista, AZ

Why spelling should count

After discussing the characteristics of jellyfish in science, I passed out a worksheet. No questions were raised so I gave myself a pat on the back for teaching so well. The next day, I graded the papers in the teachers' lounge. One question was: "The armlike structure the jellyfish uses to catch and trap fish, is a ......". Not one — but all my seventh period students answered "testicle."

After seeing this answer for the twentieth time, I hollered out in frustration, "Another testicle!" At this moment our new, MALE student-teacher walked through the lounge door. The mental picture this gave me was too much. Needless to say, seventh period had a very heavy review that day with much laughter and some explanation about why spelling counts.

— Elizabeth L. Snaiski, Mound Middle School, Decatur, IL

5. IT'S THE PRINCIPAL OF THE THING

We have maintained for years that we have never seen an exemplary school that didn't have an exemplary principal. Obviously, some of the very best principals are those who can keep their wits when everything around them is falling apart. They can take a bomb scare, a pep rally, the dreaded busses and band in stride.

Also, some of the best principals are those who refuse to take themselves or their exalted roles too seriously. Anyone who has seen the male half of this compiler team in his Big Bird suit can confirm that only the very best can maintain their dignity when wearing a large number of very yellow feathers and a big, gold beak.

The secret seems to be contained in that perpetually befuddled look that so many principals wear. You know the one. That look that makes visitors to the building think that the principal must surely be someone else new to the building in worse need of help than they, themselves, are. It is also the uncanny ability to cover a serious faux pas on the intercom with a cough, the intelligence to realize that the cafeteria is not a place to see or be seen during the lunch hour, and the common sense to laugh at any mistakes which can't be blamed on the assistant principal.

Clout where it counts

As the principal of a middle school, I had the once-in-a-lifetime experience of having both my daughters attending my school **at the same time**. During an unusually hot month of March and during the week before the North Central Accreditation team arrived to evaluate the school, I received a petition from the students requesting permission to wear shorts. Our school policy did not allow shorts and since we were busy preparing for the North Central visit, we ignored the petition.

The day the visiting team arrived, 250 students came to school wearing shorts in defiance of the policy. I announced over the intercom that the students had one period to change out of their shorts into their regular clothes. Those students who chose not to do so would report to the Cafetorium.

As I walked into the Cafetorium, the fifteen members of the North Central team were standing at the back and thirty students wearing shorts stood staring at me defiantly. Two familiar members of the "dirty thirty" were my daughters, Marci and Kara. After much discussion, the thirty students were sent home to change clothes.

As a consequence, the Student Council and Staff held a panel discussion and the "no shorts" policy was dropped. In May, Kara ran for Student Council. Her campaign slogan was straight to the point. "VOTE FOR KARA. I CAN INFLUENCE MY DAD." Needless to say , Kara won the election.

> — *Walt Grebing, Principal,*
> *Broomfield Heights Middle School,*
> *Broomfield, CO*

If the shoe fits ...

One particular middle school student was consistently late each morning. The principal finally made arrangements for a 7:00 a.m. conference with parents — no excuses. Guess who was late? The principal!

—James A. Zeedyk, Principal,
Holland Junior High School

What do students remember?

Several years ago I was teaching seventh grade science. It was customary for me to try to get a feel for the kinds of science activities the students enjoyed and remembered from the previous year by asking a few probing question. During one of these sessions I asked, "What one thing do you remember most about sixth grade science?"

Almost immediately a hand shot up and a boy blurted out, "I remember the time my sixth grade teacher's false teeth fell out of her mouth and onto the floor. I'll never forget that!" I'm sure he won't, and neither will I.

— Joseph Somers, Principal,
Medford Memorial School,
Medford, NJ

Mercy is always its own reward

Each year we take our sixth graders on a three day trip to Epcot Center and Sea World in Orlando. In order to participate students must have good conduct and exhibit "effort" in grades. Judi, unfortunately, was involved in a fight the first week of school and was suspended. That usually means no trip. However, if their behavior "turns around" for a significant period of time, they can appeal and I have to make a decision on whether or not they can go on the trip. Judi had been a model student ever since the fight and I had already decided to let her go but made her go through the process of appeal (she did not know my inclination was to let her go). If I had entertained any doubt about taking her, the last lines of her letter sealed her trip for her! I think it is **wonderful.**

Dear Ms. Hopping,

I know that I got in a fight and I regret it. But I learned my lesson and I have changed. The way you can tell I have changed is because I have been out of trouble and I have been here on time since Miss Neale told me that if I didn't want to be on in school suspension and wanted to go to Epcot that I had to be here on time. So I haven't been absent and I have been here on time. I also have kept my grades up to A, B, C, but I did get one F in Math and I plan to bring it up. I also thank you for giving me a chance and taking in consideration to let me go to Epcot. Like the Bible says "be merciful to others and God will be merciful to you and comfort you as you do others."

— Linda Hopping, Principal
Holcomb Bridge Middle School,
Alpharetta, GA

6. GOTCHA!!

Just before school starts each year, thousands of middle graders call elaborate strategy and planning sessions. Contrary to our hopes and prayers that they are getting geared up academically, they are getting geared up diabolically. Their immediate task, once school has started, is to see how quickly they can have at least one and preferably several teachers in hysterics. Their plans are devious. The scheming and plotting is worthy of an Agatha Christie novel. No detail must be overlooked. No amount of planning is too time-consuming.

The goal is to be the first student to have a teacher rant, rave, and possibly even scream in frustration. The prize is the awe and admiration of fellow students. No one is safe. Everyone is a potential victim of the dreaded "GOTCHA!!"

Let's be practical

In our transition to middle schools, I discovered that I would be teaching in the middle school my daughter attends. When I asked her how she felt about this, her response was heartwarming: "Oh Mom, that will be great!" I reached out to hug her for being so affirming when she quickly completed her thought: "I won't have to walk to school anymore."

— *Eileen Copple, Coleman Middle School, Wichita, KS*

Peer teaching

Teaching a sixth grade geography class one day, I was frustrated by my inability to convince one girl that Mexico and the United States were separate countries. Discussions of different languages, governments, monetary units, and even pointing out boundaries worked to no avail. Finally, another student asked if she could help. "Kelly," she said, "look at this map. See? Mexico is yellow. The United States is green." "Oh, I get it," Kelly responded and cheerfully sat down.

> — *Ruth Huyler Glass, The Langley School, McLean, VA*

Poetic license

A get well card from a student when the principal was in the hospital:

> I won't say that I miss you,
> for that would be a lie.
>
> I hope I'll get to see you,
> soon before you die. (I'm just kidding!)

> — *James A. Zeedyk, Principal, Holland Junior High School*

Sure, teach!

The science teacher pulled up in front of the school with a load of boxes in the back of his wagon. He started carrying the first one in, then asked a group of kids by the front door if they'd give him a hand. Without batting an eye, they all began to clap.

— *John Rowley, Heritage Junior High, Livingston, NY*

Clever, these kids

Three years ago, an eighth grade student played an unforgettable joke on me. I usually arrive early and one morning I was stopped by Garren who stated, "Mr. Bird, the guidance counselor said you are needed in the office. An emergency parent conference has been scheduled and they need you."

Garren was a trustworthy student; so I rushed to the administrative wing. On the guidance counselor's door, I found a typed note reading, "Mr. Bird, your first period class is going to be covered by a teacher on "planning" during your conference. Please be seated until the Robbins (parents) arrive."

After ten minutes of waiting I became concerned and ran to my first period class. No one was there! In panic, I checked with my neighboring teachers and . . . NO information.

Frustrated and genuinely nervous, I looked around and found another typed note. It read, "Mr. Bird's first period class is to report to the auditorium and sit in Section "B". I ran down, peeked in and saw my first period, eighth grade class in the middle of a seventh grade "reward" assembly — watching a great movie. There was nothing I could do, Garren pulled it off, on a Friday, my testing day!

— Bill Bird, DeLand Middle School,
DeLand, FL

Compassion for the teacher

I stood before my science class returning some very uninspired papers. The students were capable of so much more and I couldn't understand why they had not done better. So, I asked them why the grades weren't higher. "We're dumb! That's why."

I told them they absolutely were not dumb. "In fact", I said, "you are some of the smartest people I have ever taught. You are not dumb. Let's see. Any of you who really thinks you are dumb, stand up. Just stand up and let's see who's dumb in here."

No one stood for a few seconds and then the very brightest student in the room rose to his feet. I was astounded. "Tommy, you can't possibly think you are dumb. Why are you standing up?"

Tommy replied, "I just hated to see you standing up there all by yourself." (Gotcha!)

— Unknown contributor

It's a matter of perspective

7th grader: "Mr. B, isn't it your birthday today?"
"That's right, James."
"How old are you?" (makes face)
"28" (I was at the time)
"28! Oh God! You're almost dead."

— Stephen C. Bonnie, William Penn Charter School, Philadelphia, PA

Devious devilment

One of my fondest recollections of a prank come home to roost occurred when two of our 8th grade boys, Tim and Bart, were repaying me for a joke I had played on them. (We had a running battle going.)

One day I noticed that the whole set of our newest *World Book* was missing! In its place was a cryptic message informing me that, if I wished to retrieve it, I would need to follow the instructions on the sheet.

These instructions led me to another note, and another, until I had found a dozen of them and had been ALL OVER our three story building including the furnace room! Finally a message instructed me to go to Mrs. Cox's room (Tim's mother by the way); and there I found the encyclopedias along with the culprits who very willingly returned the books to their proper place.

They never did tell me how they had gotten them out of my media center undetected.

— Janet Hedrick, York Middle School, York, NE

A night to remember

We have an activity at El Dorado Middle School which is called "Catch Em Being Good." One person who really got caught was our assistant principal. After officiating at a basketball game in our gym, he went out to do his daily jogging. When he returned to the building, he decided to shower before he went home. He came back into the darkened building and went into the shower room. After his shower, he came out and dried his eyes so he could see.

Just as he put the towel down he looked up into the eyes of the entire girls' basketball team. We are unsure as to who was more startled, but the next day the entire faculty enjoyed putting up a big Garfield sign in the cafeteria which read "Mr. Patterson: We Caught You Being Good." Being the good natured person he is, Mr. Patterson took the whole thing in stride. But, I don't think some of the girls' basketball team will ever forget the evening.

— *Bonnie Lynch, El Dorado Middle School, El Dorado, KS*

Don't ask

During a discussion of conservation of natural resources, I questioned the class about methods for controlling soil erosion. "How do shelter belts help control soil erosion?" I asked. "They act as a wind break," Dave responded. "We should name Bobby 'shelter belt', then," added another student. "Why is that?" I questioned, curious. "Because he breaks wind better than anybody else I know."

— *Linda Omidi, Northport Middle School, Port St. Lucie, FL*

7. EXCUSES, EXCUSES, EXCUSES

Edward DeBono refers to one type of thinking as vertical, which means that every question has an answer. He prefers, however, lateral or horizontal thinking in which case thinkers come up with multiple possibilities in answer to a question. Now this isn't just the three most dreaded words a teacher can hear — answers my vary — it is the ability to see multiple ways to solve a problem.

As in so many other areas of school, we could take lessons from our students when it comes to this multiple option theory. In fact, most teachers have taken a lesson or two. The most elaborate explanation for why a task is incomplete, missing, or, better yet, stolen, is such a lesson in creativity. Those long, sad stories which inevitably end with, "and that's what really, really happened," is another.

So the next time you think a large, tall tale is merely that — a large, tall and mostly a tale — try to think of excuses, excuses, excuses as lateral, creative thinking done right before your very eyes. Some days that seems to help.

A slow learner

A student's book was left on the bus. On a paper in the book, "I will not forget my book" was written 50 times.

— James Zeedyk, Holland Jr. High

The truth hurts

Robbie came into the Guidance Office with a referral from the math teacher. Over the past few days, Robbie had not turned in his math assignments.

After asking Robbie why he had not completed his homework in several days, there was a long silence. He then replied, "Well my mom just doesn't know how to do this darn stuff."

— Mark Tobin, Pattonville Heights MS,
Maryland Heights, MO

Note to attendance officer:

Dear Mr. Carpenter:

Please excuse Teddy for being absent yesterday. He had a sour trout.

His mother

Dear Parent:

Can we excuse this child for having a bad fishing experience?

Mr. Carpenter
Attendance Clerk

— Michael Blasewitz, Walker Middle School,
Orlando, FL

Excuses, excuses!

Over the past few years we have received a number of interesting notes explaining the reasons for students' absences from school. Some of the more graphic ones include:

Please excuse....

a polar bear?

...on January 29, 30, 31, and 32. He had a cold.

...for a funeral yesterday. He was a polar bear.

...from missing school yesterday. He had loose vowels.

...for missing yesterday. He had two teeth taken out of his face.

...for missing last Friday. I took her downtown and had her shot.

...for being absent. He had a bone in his leg.

— *Susan Freepartner,*
T.T. Knight Middle School, Louisville, KY

If at first you don't succeed...

Charlie was hyperactive and extremely bright. He had a wonderful sense of humor and was my daily ray of sunshine. In my homeroom on this particular day, Charlie had used some language I didn't appreciate. During the course of the day he left three notes on my desk. The first note said:

Mrs. Perry,

I am sorry for the bad language I have been using. I hope you don't call my Mom or you won't see me tomorrow. This will give you a hint. * Here he had drawn an elaborate tombstone with the words:

Charlie
lies
here
dead

P. S. I will not do it again, I promise, and I never break a promise.

The second note:

PLEASE
one more chance today

The third note:

Dear Mrs. Perry,

Please do not call my father. I will behave for the rest of the month if you do not call him.

Sincerely,
C.

— Christine E. Perry, Sierra Vista, AZ

Embarrassing evidence

A perpetually tardy-to-school student had the gall on her sixteenth tardy to argue that she had again overslept and had rushed to school so that she would be only a few minutes late. The secretary asked several questions about the circumstance of this tardy. The student adamantly maintained her story, gasping and sighing in disbelief that all persons present would not believe her story. Gall!

With a smile, the secretary held a mirror to the student's face, clearly displaying the white powder remnants of a doughnut (or two) purchased at a nearby bakery.

Gulp...sigh...chagrin ...and the experience did prove to be the end of tardiness for this student.

— Larry Lewis, Mansfield Public Schools, Mansfield, OH

Parents should proofread too

Several years ago a student brought an excuse from home which read as follows:

"Please excuse Karen for missing school last week. Her mother had an operation and we needed someone home to help until the decision had healed."

Signed,

Her Father

— *Jerry R. Adrian, McFarland, WI*

"39 reasons why I don't have my homework"
by Matthew Doyle

"39 teacher responses"
by Mr. Connell

My brother used it for a napkin.
I've met your brother. He doesn't use napkins!

My mom threw it away.
Mothers never throw anything away.

My sister used it for a love letter.
Sister? C'mon Matt! Does your father know about this?

50

Lightning struck my book bag.
A rubber book bag???

I had the flu and couldn't do it.
The 8 hour bug?

My brother
used it to line
the bird cage.
*I'll take
it. It will
look the same
to me.*

My dad used it
as a coaster for
his beer mug.
*Send him
to A.A. meet-
ings in the
future.*

We had a power outage and that was the only paper in
the house to start a fire with.
Another toilet paper shortage?

I wrote it in disappearing ink.
You'll wish you swallowed a little yourself.

We invited a math committee over and we needed
placemats that they would like.
Great! I'm sure they'll revise the curriculum now!

I was mugged and they took all my valuables.
Nice to see they were high school dropouts.

I made it into a paper airplane and it got hijacked.
The F.B.I. has it on radar.

You said we didn't have to do it if we didn't want to.
Inferring senility here, Matt?

I'm so smart I shouldn't have to do it.
Mirror, mirror on the wall...

I don't get paid, so I shouldn't have to do it.
Have your parents raise your allowance.

It didn't look interesting enough.
*Maybe the red ink I'll use to correct it with will
brighten things up.*

I left it on your desk.
The desk snatchers are back!

My mom put poison in my breakfast, so I had to eat
my homework.
*After you get your grade, you'll realize that
breakfast would have been better.*

My dad thought it was an old newspaper and threw it
in the fireplace.
*When he gets your grade I wonder what he'll be
using for kindling then.*

A steamroller rolled it over so now it is a permanent
part of the road.
*And you didn't throw yourself in front of it to
make a rescue?*

My baby brother spilled mustard all over it.
*Brothers and sisters?!?! I guess your dad won't be
putting in long hours anymore.*

I showed it to my grandmother and she thought I was so smart, she kept it.
   A "smart" paper. Show your elders more respect!

I didn't want to embarrass the other kids in the class.
   Don't worry. You won't!

My mom thought it was a shopping list.
   I hope she brought her credit cards to cover it.

The dog ate it.
   Your dog is into garbage, eh?

My sister is on a diet and she says paper has no calories.
   Well, if she ate your homework, she had a whole bull.

Yesterday was my day off.
   Let me see your union card.

I felt so sick, I puked five times and couldn't do it.
   Take two aspirin and see me in the morning.

I fell asleep as soon as I got home.
   Drink coffee!

I was reading Huck Finn and I got so involved, I couldn't stop.
   Listen to the book on tape.

I didn't do it because I had a basketball game.
   If you were 6'9", I would overlook missing homework.

Some birds used it for a nest.
   Hmm. I can imagine what it looked like!

I'm going for the Guinness Book for the most days not handing in homework.
Let's hope you don't win.

Realizing you're a compassionate person, I didn't do it.
Boy, have you ever misread the vibes I'm giving off!

I loaned it to my best friend but he suddenly moved away.
He's your idea of a "best" friend?

My pencils were attacked by termites.
Call an exterminator.

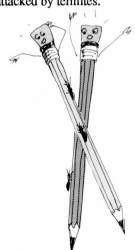

You mean to say it's not the last day of school!?!?!?
I thought you covered calendars in the 1st grade!

I did it!
April Fools!

PUBLICATIONS
National Middle School Association

A Journey Through Time: A Chronology of
Middle Level Resources Edward J. Lawton
(36 pages)...$5.00

Dynamite in the Classroom: A How-To Handbook
for Teachers Sandra L. Schurr
(272 pages) $15.00

Developing Effective Middle Schools Through
Faculty Participation. Second and Enlarged
Edition Elliot Y. Merenbloom (108 pages)...........$8.50

Preparing to Teach in Middle Level Schools
William M. Alexander and C. Kenneth McEwin
(76 pages)...$7.00

Guidance in the Middle Level Schools:
Everyone's Responsibility
Claire Cole (34 pages)......................................$5.00

Young Adolescent Development and School
Practices: Promoting Harmony
John Van Hoose & David Strahan (68 pages)............$7.00

When the Kids Come First: Enhancing Self-
Esteem James A. Beane and
Richard P. Lipka (96 pages).................................$8.00

Interdisciplinary Teaching: Why and How
Gordon F. Vars (56 pages) $6.00

Cognitive Matched Instruction in Action
Esther Fusco and Associates (36 pages)..................$5.00

The Middle School
Donald H. Eichhorn (128 pages)............................$6.00

Long-Term Teacher-Student Relationships:
A Middle School Case Study
Paul George (30 pages).......................................$4.00

Positive Discipline: A Pocketful of Ideas
William Purkey and David Strahan (56 pages)........... $6.00

**Teachers as Inquirers: Strategies for Learning
With and About Early Adolescents**
Chris Stevenson (52 pages)................................. $6.00

Adviser-Advisee Programs: Why, What, and How
Michael James (75 pages)................................... $7.00

**What Research Says to the Middle Level
Practitioner** J. Howard Johnston and Glenn C. Markle
(112   pages).. $8.00

Evidence for the Middle School
Paul George and Lynn Oldaker (52 pages)................ $6.00

Involving Parents in Middle Level Education
John W. Myers (52 pages) $6.00

Perspectives: Middle Level Education
John H. Lounsbury, Editor (190 pages)..................$10.00

**The Team Process: A Handbook for Teachers,
Second and Enlarged Edition**
Elliot Y. Merenbloom (120 pages)........................ $8.00

This We Believe NMSA Committee (24 pages)....... $3.50

Teacher to Teacher Nancy Doda (64 pages)............ $6.00

**NMSA, 4807 Evanswood Drive,
Columbus, Ohio 43229-6292
(614) 848-8211   FAX (614) 848-4301**